Best Kids' Jokes EVER!

VOLUME 1

Highlights Press
Honesdale, Pennsylvania

Cover Design by Colleen Pidell
Contributing Illustrators: David Coulson, Kelly Kennedy,
Pat N. Lewis, Neil Numberman, Rich Powell, Kevin Rechin,
Rick Stromoski, Pete Whitehead

Published by Highlights for Children
P.O. Box 18201
Columbus, Ohio 43218-0201
Printed in the United States of America

ISBN: 978-1-68437-244-7
First edition

Visit our website at Highlights.com.

10 9 8 7 6 5 4 3 2 1

CONTENTS

UP-*ROAR*-IOUS ANIMALS 5

SILLY SPORTS 16

PET PUNS 24

MUSIC AND ART 30

ON THE GO! 37

JOKES ON THE JOB 46

FAMILY HILARITY 54

WACKY WEATHER 61

FAIRY TALE TICKLERS 68

BARNYARD CHUCKLES 75

DOCTOR! DOCTOR! 83

FUNNY FOOD 91

HOLIDAY HUMOR 99

LAUGH LESSONS 120

UP-*ROAR*-IOUS ANIMALS

What do cheetahs like to eat?

Fast food.

What is an ape's favorite cookie?

Chocolate chimp.

What sound do porcupines make when they kiss?

"Ouch!"

How do you make a squid laugh?

With ten-tickles.

What does a spider do when he gets angry?

He goes up the wall.

How does a lion greet the other animals on the savannah?

"Pleased to eat you."

Marielle: I know someone who thinks he's an owl.

Brett: Who?

Marielle: Make that two people.

Why do giraffes have long necks?

Because their feet smell.

What do you do with a blue whale?

Cheer it up.

Why do pandas like old movies?

Because they're in black and white.

A snail was climbing up a cherry tree when a beetle spotted it. "Hey," said the beetle, "there aren't any cherries on that tree yet."
"I know," replied the snail, "but there will be by the time I get up there."

How does a tiger paddle a canoe?

He uses his roar.

Who did the deer invite to his birthday party?

His nearest and deer-est friends.

What game do mice play?

Hide-and-squeak.

Knock, knock.

Who's there?

Aurora.

Aurora who?

Aurora's just come from that big polar bear.

What is a llama's favorite drink?

Llama-nade.

Why do sea horses only like salt water?

Because pepper water makes them sneeze.

What do you get when you cross a caterpillar and a parrot?

A walkie-talkie.

If the alphabet goes from A to Z, what goes from Z to A?

A zebra.

What kind of turtles are green and easy to see?

Green sea turtles.

Cory: Have you ever seen a fish cry?

Tory: No, but I have seen a whale blubber.

Why did the bear get so scared?

He looked in the mirror.

Why is a giraffe a bad dinner guest?

It eats, leaves.

What is a shark's favorite game?

Swallow the leader.

How do you stop a skunk from smelling?

You hold its nose.

What is green and can jump a mile in a minute?

A grasshopper with hiccups.

Gorilla keeper: My gorilla is sick. Do you know a good animal doctor?

Zookeeper: No, I'm afraid all the doctors I know are people.

What did the otter say to his sister, who just pulled a prank on him?

"This is otterly ridiculous."

What type of snake builds things?

A boa constructor.

What is the saddest bird?

The blue jay.

What did the cashier say when she saw the giraffe standing in line?

"Necks!"

What do you call an exploding monkey?

A ba-boom.

What's the best thing to do if an elephant sneezes?

Get out of its way!

Knock, knock.

Who's there?

Lion.

Lion who?

Lion on your doorstep. Open up!

Why does the ocean roar?

You would, too, if you had lobsters in your bed.

How can you tell a water buffalo from a mouse?

Try to pick it up. If you can't, it's a water buffalo.

Where do funny frogs sit?

On silly pads.

Why don't cheetahs ever take baths?

Because they don't want to be spotless.

What does a hippo get if he stops shaving?

A hippopata-mustache.

First firefly: You've gotten taller since I last saw you.

Second firefly: I guess I'm having a glow spurt!

Where do you find polar bears?

It depends on where you lost them.

What do you call two octopuses that look alike?

I-tentacle twins.

What animal hates cold feet?

A mother kangaroo.

Why does a flamingo stand on one leg?

If it lifted both legs, it would fall over!

A duck, a deer, and a skunk went out to dinner. When the waiter brought the check, the deer said he didn't have a buck, and the skunk said he didn't have a scent. So they put it on the duck's bill!

Why can't you take a picture of a tiger with a hat?

Because you can't take a picture with a hat!

What goes *zzub, zzub*?

A bee flying backwards.

Olivia: I saw a man-eating shark in the zoo aquarium.

Seamus: That's nothing. I saw a girl eating shrimp in the zoo restaurant.

What state do lions like best?

Maine.

What did the wolf say when someone stepped on his foot?

"Aoooowwwwww!"

What did the bus driver say to the frog?

"Hop on!"

Joe: What do you call a truck full of bison?

Danny: I have no clue.

Joe: A buffa-load!

Why don't giraffes ever learn how to swim?

Because it's easier just to walk on the bottom of the pool.

What do you call a rhino at the North Pole?

Lost.

SILLY SPORTS

What kind of bees are bad at football?

Fumblebees.

Why don't fish like to play basketball?

They're afraid of the net.

How do monkeys stay in shape?

They go to the jungle gym.

What is the loudest kind of sports equipment?

A racket.

Knock, knock.

Who's there?

Ratio.

Ratio who?

Ratio to the end of the street!

How do basketball players stay cool during the game?

They stand close to the fans.

Why did the golfer wear two pairs of pants?

In case he got a hole in one.

Teacher: Cameron, what are the four seasons?

Cameron: Baseball, football, hockey, and vacation!

Why was the piano tuner hired to play on the baseball team?

Because he had perfect pitch.

What is the quietest game in the world?

Bowling—you can hear a pin drop.

What is harder to catch the faster you run?

Your breath.

Why did the football coach send in his second string?

To tie up the game.

Baseball player: How do I exit the stadium?

Umpire: Three strikes and you're out.

What is an insect's favorite sport?

Cricket.

Which athletes are the sloppiest eaters?

Basketball players, because they dribble so much.

In what sport do you sit down going up and stand up going down?

Skiing.

What do you call a boomerang that doesn't come back to you?

A bummerang.

What goes around a field but does not move?

A fence.

What do championship football players eat their cereal in?

Super bowls.

Knock, knock.

Who's there?

Avery.

Avery who?

Avery time I swing at a bad pitch, I strike out.

How does a sneaker sneeze?

"A tennis shoe! A tennis shoe!"

What does outer space have in common with basketball?

They both have shooting stars.

Knock, knock.

Who's there?

Andy.

Andy who?

Andy shoots, Andy scores!

What has four legs and catches flies?

Two outfielders.

What dog can play football?

A golden receiver.

What do you get if you cross a newborn snake with a basketball?

A bouncing baby boa.

If you were running a race, and you passed the person in second place, what place would you be in?

You would be in second; you passed the person in second place, not first.

How is a baseball team like a pancake?

They both need a good batter.

What do you do if the basketball court gets flooded?

Call in the subs.

How do you make a cream puff?

Take it jogging.

Why did the ghost get kicked out of the football game?

Because he screamed, "Boo!"

Alexis: I wish I could bowl as well as I can bat.

Leah: How well can you bat?

Alexis: All I ever get are strikes!

When is a baby good at basketball?

When it's dribbling.

What do you call a pig that plays basketball?

A ball hog.

Knock, knock.

Who's there?

Falafel.

Falafel who?

I falafel my bike and hurt my knee.

What is the hardest thing about learning how to skate?

The ground.

What did the glove say to the baseball?

"Catch you later!"

What should you drink when you're watching your favorite sports game?

Root beer.

Why did the triangle jog around the block?

To get into shape.

PET PUNS

What did the cat say when he stubbed his toe?

"Me-ow!"

What dog loves to take bubble baths?

A shampoodle.

Which U.S. state do cats and dogs like to visit?

Petsylvania.

What do you call a cat that drank too much lemonade?

A sourpuss.

What is a rabbit's favorite game?

Hopscotch.

What do snakes do after they argue?

They hiss and make up.

Kate: Did you like the story about the dog that ran two miles just to pick up a stick?

Nate: No, I thought it was a little far-fetched.

What did the Dalmatian say after eating?

"That hit the spots!"

What's orange and sounds like a parrot?

A carrot.

What is a dog's favorite movie?

Jurassic Bark.

Tara: Did you give the goldfish fresh water today?

Jackson: No. They didn't finish the water I gave them yesterday.

What position does a dog play on the football field?

Rufferee.

What do you get when you cross a tarantula with a rose?

I'm not sure, but I wouldn't try smelling it!

Why do you have to be careful when it's raining cats and dogs?

So you don't step in a poodle.

Where does a hamster go on vacation?

Hamsterdam.

What kind of pet can't be found at a pet store?

A trumpet.

Which bones do dogs not like?

Trombones.

Audrey: My pet turtle turned two today!

Malcolm: Cool! Are you going to shell-ebrate his birthday?

Is it bad luck if a black cat follows you?

It depends on whether you're a person or a mouse.

What did one flea say to the other flea?

"Should we walk or take the dog?"

What do you call it when it's raining cats?

A down-purr.

Ozzie: How much birdseed should I buy?

Store clerk: How many birds do you have?

Ozzie: None, but I want to grow some.

What do you get when you cross a dog and a dandelion?

A collie-flower.

What happened when the cat ate a ball of yarn?

She had mittens.

What did the boy say when his dog ran away?

"Well, doggone!"

What is a snake's favorite river?

The Hississippi.

Blake: My dog's the smartest in town. He can say his own name in perfect English.

Alice: What's his name?

Blake: Ruff.

Why did the dog leap for joy?

Joy was holding the cookies.

MUSIC AND ART

What is a cow's favorite painting?

The Moona Lisa.

Why do opera singers make good sailors?

They know how to handle high C's.

What do artists use when they are sleepy?

Crayawns.

What did the conductor say to the orchestra?

"We've got a score to settle."

Band student: Our school played Beethoven last night.

Gym student: Who won?

Why could the artist cross the bridge whenever he wanted to?

Because it was a drawbridge.

What kind of music do balloons hate?

Pop.

What did the painting say to the detective?

"It wasn't me, I was framed!"

Jill: Was that you singing when I came in?

Jan: Yes. I was killing time before my lesson.

Jill: Well, you were definitely using the right weapon.

What's the only music a mummy listens to?

Wrap.

What rock group has four men that don't sing?

Mount Rushmore.

Allison: Will you draw me a horse and buggy?

Artist: OK.

Allison: You only drew the horse.

Artist: I thought the horse would draw the buggy.

Why do bagpipers march when they play?

To get away from the noise.

What color is the wind?

Blew.

Why were the musical notes upset?

Because they were right next to the trouble clef.

Why did the robot win the dance contest?

He was a dancing machine.

Why did Mozart get rid of his chickens?

They kept saying, "Bach, Bach, Bach."

Knock, knock.

Who's there?

Statue.

Statue who?

It's me. Statue?

What's green and smells like blue paint?

Green paint.

If lightning strikes an orchestra, who is most likely to get hit?

The conductor.

What did Michelangelo say to the ceiling?

"I got you covered."

Phil: Santa decided to give his reindeer a year off, so he got eight monkeys to pull his sleigh— Do, Re, Fa, So, La, Ti, and Do.

Will: What about Mi?

Phil: Oh, are you a monkey, too?

Where do crayons go on vacation?

Colorado.

What do musicians do when they lose their beat?

They have a tempo-tantrum.

Two windmills are standing in a field. One asks the other, "What kind of music do you like?"

The other one says, "I'm a big metal fan."

What's noisier than a whooping crane?

A trumpeting swan.

When is a tuba good for your teeth?

When it's a tuba toothpaste.

What is a skeleton's favorite instrument?

A trombone.

What has lots of keys but can't open doors?

A piano.

What kind of band doesn't play music?

A rubber band.

What kind of music do hammocks like?

Rock.

How does a tree draw a person?

It makes a stick figure.

Knock, knock.

Who's there?

Yellow.

Yellow who?

Yellow, and how are you doing today?

Where did the monster musician stay while he was on vacation?

The Vile Inn.

What do you call an imaginary color?

A pigment of your imagination.

Why do hummingbirds hum?

They forgot the words.

How do you get 27 kids to carve a statue?

Just have everybody chip in.

ON THE GO!

What kind of snake keeps its car the cleanest?

A windshield viper.

Where are the Great Plains?

At the great airports.

What will the school for race cars do after the summer?

Re-zoom.

When does the road get angry?

When someone crosses it.

Trinity: What do you get when you cross a bear and a skunk?

Kristy: I don't know. What?

Trinity: I don't know either, but it can easily get a seat on the bus!

Why couldn't the bicycle stand up by itself?

It was two tired.

Two wrongs do not make a right. But what do two rights make?

The first airplane.

What kind of truck do pigs drive?

An eighteen-squealer.

Knock, knock.

Who's there?

Lucinda.

Lucinda who?

Lucinda strap on my bike helmet—it's too tight!

What did the boy get when he leaned over the back of the boat?

A stern warning.

What did the spider do when he got a new car?

He took it out for a spin.

How do rabbits travel?

By hare-plane.

A family of pickles is about to drive across the country for a vacation.

Baby Pickle: What if we have car trouble?

Mom Pickle: It'll be OK. We'll just dill with it!

How can you drive two thousand miles with a flat tire?

Your spare tire is flat—the four you're riding on are fine.

What kind of bagel can fly?

A plain bagel.

What do lazy dogs do?

They chase parked cars.

What kind of locomotive needs a tissue?

An ah-choo-choo train.

What kind of bus has two floors and says, "Quack"?

A double ducker.

What do you call a snail on a ship?

A snailer.

Knock, knock.

Who's there?

Despair.

Despair who?

Despair tire is flat.

Where do cars go on vacation?

Key West.

What do ghosts have in the seats of their cars?

Sheet belts.

Why do tires get upset when they go bowling?

Because they never make strikes, just spares.

Passenger on plane: Those people down there look like ants!

Flight attendant: They are ants. We haven't left the ground yet.

What does a car wear on its head?

A gas cap.

Where do race cars go to wash their clothes?

The laundry vroom.

Why did the kid study in the airplane?

He wanted a higher education.

Knock, knock.

Who's there?

Jethro.

Jethro who?

Jethro the boat and stop asking questions.

What lives in the sea and carries a lot of people?

An octo-bus.

Tyler: I just flew in from Philadelphia.

Dylan: Wow! Your arms must be tired.

How are a train and an orchestra alike?

They both have conductors.

How can you tell a school bus from a grape?

Jump on one for a while. If you don't get any juice, it's a school bus.

What did the car wheels say after a long drive?

"We're tired out!"

Nina: What happened to the wooden car with the wooden wheels and the wooden engine?

Paige: I don't know. What?

Nina: It wooden go!

What's the difference between a jeweler and a ship's captain?

One sees the watches, and the other watches the seas.

Why did the pioneers cross the country in covered wagons?

Because they didn't want to wait forty years for a train.

Who un-invented the airplane?

The Wrong brothers.

What did the dog say to the car?

"Hey, you're in my barking spot!"

Mom: Why didn't you take the school bus home?

Andy: I tried, but it wouldn't fit in my backpack.

What flavor of ice cream do bikers like the least?

Rocky road.

What would happen if all the cars in the country were painted pink?

It would be a pink car nation.

Knock, knock.

Who's there?

Wheel.

Wheel who?

Wheel be going now. Good-bye!

JOKES ON THE JOB

What did the judge say when a skunk walked
into his courtroom?

"Odor in the court!"

Why did the lion spit out the clown?

Because he tasted funny.

What illness can you catch from a martial-arts expert?

Kung flu.

Why did the journalist go to the ice-cream parlor?

She wanted to get the scoop.

Val: Did you hear about the scientist who was reading a book about helium?

Vincent: Yes. He just couldn't put it down.

What do you call a snake that works for the government?

A civil serpent.

Why did the baker stop making doughnuts?

He got tired of the hole business.

Who are the police of the fruit world?

The apri-cops.

How do sailors get their clothes clean?

They throw them overboard. Then they are washed ashore.

Knock, knock.

Who's there?

Waiter.

Waiter who?

Waiter minute while I tie my shoes.

How do you get a baby astronaut to sleep?

You rocket.

Why are cowboys bad at math?

They're always rounding things up.

Why do ballerinas wear tutus?

Three-threes are too big and one-ones are too small.

What did the police dog say to the speeder?

"Stop in the name of the paw!"

Businessman: Well, Plan A failed. Is Plan B any good?

Businesswoman: If Plan B were any good, we would have called it Plan A.

Stella: So you're going to start a bakery?

Heidi: Yes, if I can raise the dough.

What do chess players have for breakfast?

Pawn-cakes.

What did the janitor say when he jumped out of the closet?

"Supplies!"

What bird never goes to the barber?

A bald eagle.

49

The clerk at the butcher shop is five feet ten inches tall and wears size thirteen sneakers. What does he weigh?

Meat.

What did the limestone say to the geologist?

"Don't take me for granite."

What kind of cheese do teachers put on their pizza?

Graded cheese.

What are a plumber's least favorite shoes?

Clogs.

Why did the farmer throw vegetables on the ground?

He wanted peas on Earth.

Customer: Can you help me out?

Cashier: Why, sure. Which way did you come in?

What did the judge say to the dentist?

"Do you swear to tell the tooth, the whole tooth, and nothing but the tooth?"

Why was the scientist's head wet?

Because he had a brainstorm.

Where do superheroes shop?

At the supermarket.

What do bakers put on their beds?

Cookie sheets.

Why did the comedian go out of business?

His jokes didn't make any cents.

Magician: I can turn a handkerchief into a flower.

Roger: That's nothing. I can walk down the street and turn into an alley.

Knock, knock.

Who's there?

Diploma.

Diploma who?

Diploma is here to fix de leak.

Where does a lumberjack go to buy things?

The chopping center.

What kind of gum do scientists chew?

Ex-spearmint gum.

How many bricks did the mason need to finish the building?

Just the last one.

First astronaut: What's that thing in the pan?

Second astronaut: It's an unidentified frying object

Why didn't the rocket have a job?

Because it was fired.

How does the man in the moon get his hair cut?

Eclipse it.

Why are police officers the strongest people in the world?

Because they can hold up traffic with one hand.

FAMILY HILARITY

What did the boy with the world's greatest mom do?

He built her a mom-ument.

What did the snake say to his little sister?

"Stop being such a rattle-tail!"

Who is married to Antarctica?

Uncle Arctica.

What did the cook name his son?

Stew.

Dad: Would you like an apple?

Clara: I don't feel like an apple today.

Dad: That's good. You don't look like an apple either.

What did the gorilla call his wife?

His prime mate.

Knock, knock.

Who's there?

Who's.

Who's who?

You're the dad and I'm the son!

Sister: I can make you say "purple."

Brother: No, you can't!

Sister: OK, say the colors of the American flag.

Brother: Red, white, and blue.

Sister: That's right.

Brother: But you said you'd make me say "purple."

Sister: There, you just said it!

What do you call a ghost's mother and father?

Trans-parents.

What's another name for a grandfather clock?

An old-timer.

Mom: Tommy, please pick up your room.

Tommy: I don't think I'm strong enough.

Why didn't the cub leave his mommy?

He couldn't bear it!

What did the hamburger name its daughter?

Patty.

Eli: Why does your grandmother have roller skates on her rocking chair?

Emily: She likes to rock and roll.

Knock, knock.

Who's there?

Ammonia.

Ammonia who?

Ammonia little kid!

What do you give a sick relative?

Auntie-biotics.

What is a baby's motto?

"If at first you don't succeed, cry, cry again."

Dad: What does IDK mean?

Mitch: I don't know.

Dad: You're the fifth person I've asked. Nobody knows what it means!

Why did the dad have to go to school?

To take his pop quiz.

Why was the little apple so excited?

He was going to see his Granny Smith.

Brother: Do you have holes in your socks?

Sister: No.

Brother: Then how do you get your feet in them?

Knock, knock.

Who's there?

Aunt Lou.

Aunt Lou who?

Aunt Lou do you think you are?

Dad: What was that loud noise?

Hari: My jacket fell on the floor.

Dad: Why would your jacket falling make such a loud noise?

Hari: Because I was wearing it.

Why was it easy to celebrate Mother's Day in ancient Egypt?

Because there were so many mummies.

What does a dog call his father?

Paw.

Little Brother: Do you want to hear a long joke?

Big Brother: Sure.

Little Brother: Jooooooooke.

Why does the mom carry the baby?

Because the baby can't carry the mom.

What did the boy use to keep track of his mother?

A ther-mom-eter.

Julia: Mom! There's a monster under my bed!

Mom: Tell him to get back in the closet where he belongs.

WACKY WEATHER

What is worse than raining cats and dogs?

Hailing taxis.

Why does lightning shock people?

Because it doesn't know how to conduct itself.

What song do penguins sing on a birthday?

"Freeze a Jolly Good Fellow."

Knock, knock.

Who's there?

Lorraine.

Lorraine who?

Lorraine is falling. Where's my umbrella?

What do you call it when your dog sheds all over the couch?

A hair-icane.

What did summer say to spring?

"Help, I'm going to fall!"

What kind of bow can't be tied?

A rainbow.

Why do birds fly south for the winter?

Because it's too far to walk.

Knock, knock.

Who's there?

August.

August who?

August of wind almost blew me away!

What is a bird's favorite drink?

Hot cuckoo.

What do polar bears do on the computer?

They surf the Winternet.

What is the opposite of a hurricane?

A him-icane.

What do you get when you cross a bear with a rain cloud?

A drizzly bear.

How do snowmen travel around?

By icicle.

Brianna: You won't believe what happened today.

Andrew: What?

Brianna: The weather forecast said it was going to be chilly, so my brother ran outside with a bowl and said, "Where's the chili?"

What triangles are the coldest?

Ice-osceles.

What does a rain cloud wear under its clothes?

Thunderwear.

Knock, knock.

Who's there?

Scold.

Scold who?

Scold outside.

The little tree got worried in October because all his leaves fell off. But when spring came, he was re-leaved.

What do you call a bird that stays up north during winter?

A brrrrrd.

Why was the moon acting so loony?

It was going through a phase.

Knock, knock.

Who's there?

Butter.

Butter who?

Butter bring an umbrella—it looks like rain.

What is a tornado's favorite game?

Twister.

What did one snowman say to the other?

"Is it me, or do you smell carrots?"

Jason: What would you do if you were trapped on an iceberg?

Jerome: Just chill.

Knock, knock.

Who's there?

Dancer.

Dancer who?

Dancer is simple; it wasn't a ghost—it was only the wind!

What did one hurricane say to the other?

"I have my eye on you."

How do you find out the weather when you're on vacation?

Look out the window.

Teacher: Harly, please give me the definition of climate.

Harly: That's what a kid does when he sees a tree!

What did one raindrop say to the other?

"Two's company. Three's a cloud."

What time of year is it best to use a trampoline?

In the springtime.

Knock, knock.

Who's there?

Sombrero.

Sombrero who?

Sombrero-ver the rainbow.

Why is England the wettest country?

Because the queen has reigned there for years.

What is a turtle's favorite thing to wear in winter?

A turtleneck.

What did Benjamin Franklin say when he flew a kite in a lightning storm?

Nothing—he was too shocked.

FAIRY TALE TICKLERS

How do slugs begin their fairy tales?

"Once upon a slime . . ."

What does every tarantula wish he had?

A hairy godmother.

What did the wizard say to his girlfriend?

"You look wanderful tonight."

What do you call a fairy that needs a bath?

Stinkerbell.

Knock, knock.

Who's there?

Dragon.

Dragon who?

These jokes are dragon on and on.

What do you call a king's sore throat?

A royal pain in the neck.

How much does a pirate pay to get his ears pierced?

A buccaneer.

Where did people dance in medieval times?

In knight clubs.

What is beautiful, gray, and wears glass slippers?

Cinder-elephant.

What did the King of Hearts say to the King of Spades?

"Let's make a deal."

What is a camel's favorite nursery rhyme?

Humpty Dumpty.

Where do you find the most famous dragons?

In the Hall of Flame.

Who is the king of the classroom?

The ruler.

What is a myth?

A female moth.

How does a lump of coal start a story?

"Once upon a mine . . ."

What did Cinderella say when her pictures didn't arrive?

"Someday my prints will come."

Knock, knock.

Who's there?

Fairy.

Fairy who?

Fairy pleased to meet you!

What is a knight's favorite food?

Swordfish.

Who is the king of the insects?

The monarch butterfly.

Who is the smartest fairy in Neverland?

Thinkerbell.

Why did Humpty Dumpty have a great fall?

To make up for a miserable summer.

Would Little Miss Muffet share her curds?

No whey!

Would Little Miss Muffet share her whey?

Of curds she would!

Why did the monster need braces?

Because he had an ogre-bite.

What did the pirate say on his 80th birthday?

"Aye, matey!"

How do you find King Arthur in the dark?

With a knight light.

What do you call a wizard from outer space?

A flying sorcerer.

Where do kings and queens get crowned?

On their heads.

Knock, knock.

Who's there?

Vaughn.

Vaughn who?

Vaughn day my prince will come.

How does a mermaid call a friend?

On her shell phone.

Why did the queen go to the dentist?

To get crowns on her teeth.

What was Camelot?

A place to park camels.

What does a sea monster eat for dinner?

Fish and ships.

Why did the pirate walk the plank?

He couldn't afford a dog.

What did the knight's tombstone say?

"Rust in peace."

What makes the tooth fairy so smart?

Wisdom teeth.

How did the grandmother knit a suit of armor?

She used steel wool.

Why does Tinkerbell always fly around?

Because she lives in Neverland.

Why are pirates called pirates?

They just arrrrr.

Why is Cinderella so bad at sports?

Because she has a pumpkin for a coach and runs away from the ball.

BARNYARD CHUCKLES

How do you make a milkshake?

Give a cow a pogo stick.

When did the duck wake up this morning?

At the quack of dawn.

What happens when a cow doesn't shave?

He gets a moostache.

Why did the horse eat with his mouth open?

It had bad stable manners.

Why did the sheep jump over the moon?

Because the cow was on vacation.

Colin: You should never insult a chicken.

Stacey: OK. Why not?

Colin: It's just bad cluck!

Knock, knock.

Who's there?

Goat.

Goat who?

Goat to the door and find out.

Why did the farmer name his pig Ink?

Because it always ran out of the pen.

Why did the cow say "boo"?

She had a stuffy nose.

How did the farmer find his daughter when she was lost?

He tractor.

Pig: Why are you eating alphabet soup?

Cow: Because if I were eating number soup, I'd be a cow-culator!

What kind of pictures do sheep like to paint?

Lambscapes.

Leah: Did you hear about the magic tractor?

Levi: What about it?

Leah: It turned into a field.

What is the definition of a farmer?

Someone who is outstanding in his field.

What wakes up a rooster?

An alarm clock-a-doodle-doo.

Teacher: Name five things that contain milk.

Sandra: Five cows.

Knock, knock.

Who's there?

Chesterfield.

Chesterfield who?

Chesterfield full of cows.

Laura: What new crop did the farmer plant this year?

Lee: Beets me!

Why shouldn't you tell a secret on a farm?

Because the potatoes have eyes and the corn has ears.

What animal always sleeps with its shoes on?

A horse.

What does a cow use to cut grass?

A lawn moo-er.

What do you get when you play tug-of-war with a pig?

Pulled pork.

What does a polite cow greet someone?

"How do you moo?"

Andy: I just bought a farm, and I can't decide which to buy first—a tractor or a cow.

Chuck: You'd look pretty silly riding around on a cow.

Andy: I'd look even sillier trying to milk a tractor.

What do horses do at bedtime?

They hit the hay.

Where do cows go on vacation?

Moo York, sometimes Moo Jersey.

How does a chicken tell time?

One o'cluck, two o'cluck, three o'cluck . . .

Knock, knock.

Who's there?

Rosa.

Rosa who?

Rosa corn grow in the field.

Why did the pig take a bath?

The farmer said, "Hogwash!"

What happens to a cow when it stands out in the rain?

It gets wet.

Farmer: Are you a horse? Yea or nay?

Horse: Neighhhh!

Farmer: Then I guess you're not a horse!

A rancher had 196 cows in field, but when he rounded them up, he had 200.

What has four legs and says, "Oom, oom"?

A cow walking backwards.

What happened when the pigpen broke?

The pig used a pencil.

What is a scarecrow's favorite fruit?

Strawberries.

Knock, knock.

Who's there?

Cows.

Cows who?

Cows say "moo," not "who."

Tina: I just heard that Bill bought a farm a mile long and an inch wide.

Sam: Really? What could he grow on a farm that size?

Tina: Spaghetti.

What does it mean when you find a horseshoe?

Some poor horse is walking around in just his socks.

When does a cow have eight legs?

When there are two cows.

What do you call people who like tractors?

Protractors.

DOCTOR! DOCTOR!

Why did the pony go to the doctor?

Because he was a little horse.

How did the bird get to the doctor's office?

He flu.

What has two holes, no legs, and runs?

A nose.

Why did Dracula go to the doctor?

He was coffin.

Knock, knock.

Who's there?

Anita.

Anita who?

Anita tissue.

Knock, knock.

Who's there?

Tish.

Tish who?

Why, yes, I'd love a tissue.

Nurse: Doctor, there's a ghost in the waiting room.

Doctor: Tell him I can't see him.

If an apple a day keeps the doctor away, what does an onion a day do?

It keeps everyone away.

What kind of illness can a zebra get?

Stripe throat.

Doctor: What brings you to my office today?

Squirrel: I just realized that I am what I eat. Nuts!

What wild animal might you find in a dentist's office?

A molar bear.

Why did the book go to the doctor?

It hurt its spine.

Where did the soda go when it lost its bubbles?

To the fizzician.

What do you give to a sick lemon?

Lemon aid.

Man: Doctor! Doctor! I need some glasses!

Waiter: You sure do. This is a restaurant.

Where do boats go when they are sick?

To the dock.

What do you call a dog that has the flu?

A germy shepherd.

What do you get if you eat uranium?

Atomic ache.

What did one elevator say to the other?

"I think I'm coming down with something."

Why did the cookie go to the doctor?

It felt crumby.

What did the doctor say to the woman who swallowed a spoon?

"Sit still and don't stir."

What vitamin do fish take?

Vitamin sea.

Patient: Doctor, what should I do when my ear rings?

Doctor: Answer it!

Knock, knock.

Who's there?

Eyes.

Eyes who?

Eyes better come in before I catch a cold.

What do you give a sick bird?

Tweetment.

What did the doctor give the pig for its rash?

Oinkment.

Patient: Nurse, Nurse! I was playing my harmonica, and I swallowed it.

Nurse: You're lucky you weren't playing a piano!

Where do bees go when they get hurt?

To the waspital.

Which state needs a handkerchief?

Mass-ACHOO!-setts.

What do you give to a puppy that has a fever?

Mustard—it's the best thing for a hot dog.

Knock, knock.

Who's there?

Stan.

Stan who?

Stan back. I think I'm going to sneeze.

Where does bacteria go on vacation?

Germany.

What did the doctor say to the frog?

"You need a hoperation."

What do you get if you eat pasta while you're sick?

Macaroni and sneeze.

Ben: Doctor, it hurts when I touch here and here and here. What's wrong with me?

Doctor: Your finger is broken.

Patient: Doctor, Doctor, I feel like a set of curtains!

Doctor: Well, pull yourself together.

Why did the Dalmatian go to the eye doctor?

Because he was seeing spots.

Why did the banana go to the doctor?

Because it wasn't peeling well.

What should you do if you break your arm in two places?

Stay away from those places.

FUNNY FOOD

Knock, knock.

Who's there?

Distressing.

Distressing who?

Distressing has too much vinegar.

Sue: What are we having for dinner?

Jim: Oh, hundreds of things.

Sue: Good! What are they?

Jim: Beans!

A tomato, some lettuce, and some water were in a race. The water was running, the lettuce was a head, and the tomato was trying to ketchup.

Knock, knock.

Who's there?

Stew.

Stew who?

Stew early to go to bed.

What is the laziest food ever?

Bread—it just loafs around.

What is a camera's favorite kind of sandwich?

Cheese.

What dip do bath towels eat at parties?

Shower cream and onion.

Why should you knock before you open the refrigerator?

Because you might see the salad dressing.

Why did the bacon laugh?

Because the egg cracked a yolk.

What do Hawaiian pumpkins say?

"Happy Hulaween!"

Rosey: Which do you like better, salt or pepper?

Stephanie: Pepper.

Rosey: What? How in-salt-ing!

What do you call rotten eggs, rotten fruit, and spoiled milk in a bag?

Grosseries.

Why did the monkey eat so many bananas?

He liked them a bunch.

Where do hamburgers dance?

At a meatball.

Knock, knock.

Who's there?

Almond.

Almond who?

Almond the other side of the door.

How do you make hot dogs shiver?

Put chili beans on them.

What is Dracula's favorite coffee?

Decoffinated.

What is a dog's favorite kind of pepper?

Howlapeño.

What's worse than finding a worm in your apple?

Finding half a worm in your apple.

What happens when you tell an egg a great joke?

It cracks up.

Diner: Waiter, this food tastes funny.

Waiter: Then why aren't you laughing?

What kind of room has no doors, no windows, and no walls?

A mushroom.

What does a sweet potato wear to bed?

Its yammies.

What is the most adorable vegetable?

The cutecumber.

Knock, knock.

Who's there?

Paris.

Paris who?

A Paris good, but I'd rather have an orange.

Why did the lettuce win the race?

He was a head.

What kind of fish goes well with peanut butter?

A jellyfish.

A ham sandwich walked into a restaurant and said, "May I have some chili with cheese?" The waiter replied, "Sorry, we don't serve food here."

What kind of nut doesn't have a shell?

A doughnut.

How do you fix a broken pizza?

With tomato paste.

What do you call a shivering glass of milk?

A milkshake.

Jonah: There are only two things I can't eat for breakfast.

Jillian: Really? What are they?

Jonah: Lunch and dinner.

How do you make a hot dog stand?

Take away its chair.

How do you make an egg roll?

You push it.

What cheese is made backward?

Edam.

Diner: Waiter, I'm in a hurry. Will the pancakes be long?

Waiter: No, they'll be round.

Knock, knock.

Who's there?

Sultan.

Sultan who?

Sultan pepper.

What is a skunk's favorite sandwich?

Peanut butter and smelly.

What does a cookie say when it's excited?

"Chip, chip, hooray!"

Why did the boy throw the butter out the window?

To see the butterfly.

What does a duck eat with soup?

Quackers.

HOLIDAY HUMOR

Knock, knock.

Who's there?

Carrot.

Carrot who?

Don't you carrot all about me?

Valentine's Day

Knock, knock.

Who's there?

Isolate.

Isolate who?

Isolate to the Valentine's Day party!

What do you call two spiders that just got married?

Newlywebs.

What did the carpet salesman give to his wife for Valentine's Day?

Rugs and kisses.

What did one leaf say to the other leaf?

"I'm falling for you."

What did the boy octopus say to the girl octopus?

"I want to hold your hand, hand, hand, hand, hand, hand, hand, hand."

What do you call a dog's kiss?

A pooch smooch.

What did the mom volcano say to the kid volcano?

"I lava you."

Romeo: Juliet, dearest, I am burning with love for you.

Juliet: Come now, Romeo, don't make a fuel of yourself.

Why did the teacher fall in love with the janitor?

Because he swept her off her feet.

What is the most affectionate animal in the sea?

A cuddlefish.

What did the farmer give his wife on Valentine's Day?

Hogs and kisses.

What did the painter say to her boyfriend?

"I love you with all my art!"

Teacher: Joe, please give me a sentence that uses the word "buoyant."

Joe: The girl ant was in love with the boy ant.

Knock, knock.

Who's there?

Mary.

Mary who?

Mary me, please! I love you!

What did the snake give his wife?

A goodnight hiss.

What do you call two birds that fell in love?

Tweethearts.

What did one pickle say to the other pickle?

"You mean a great dill to me."

Where do rabbits go after their wedding?

On their bunnymoon.

St. Patrick's Day

Knock, knock.

Who's there?

Irish.

Irish who?

Irish you a happy St. Patrick's Day!

What do you call a fake Irish stone?

A shamrock.

What do you get when you cross poison ivy with a four-leaf clover?

A rash of good luck.

What is at the end of a rainbow?

The letter W.

Where can you always find gold?

In the dictionary.

Why shouldn't you iron a four-leaf clover?

You don't want to press your luck.

April Fools' Day

Why is everyone so tired on April 1?

Because they just had a thirty-one-day March.

What do you call a mischievous egg?

A practical yolker.

What happened when the jester fell in the pond?

He got joking wet.

Where do pranksters go to eat lunch?

The laugh-eteria.

What famous inventor loved practical jokes?

Benjamin Pranklin.

What is a joker's favorite snack?

Peanut riddle.

What baseball team does a jokester like best?

The New York Prankees.

Easter

Knock, knock.

Who's there?

Esther.

Esther who?

Esther Bunny.

Knock, knock.

Who's there?

Stella.

Stella who?

Stella 'nother Esther Bunny.

Where does the Easter Bunny get his eggs?

From eggplants.

What kind of bunny can't hop?

A chocolate one.

What does the Easter Bunny get for making a basket?

Two points, just like anyone else.

What are the most difficult beans to grow?

Jelly beans.

Why do we paint Easter eggs?

Because it's easier than trying to wallpaper them.

Big Brother: All of my chocolate eggs have disappeared. What happened?

Little Brother: I don't know!

Big Brother: I need an eggs-planation.

What happened when the Easter Bunny met the love of his life?

They lived hoppily ever after.

How do you catch the Easter Bunny?

Hide in the bushes and make a noise like a carrot.

What is a rabbit's favorite candy?

Lollihops.

Fourth of July

What does the president use to decorate the White House for the Fourth of July?

The Decorations of Independence.

What's the difference between a duck and George Washington?

A duck has a bill on its face, and George Washington has his face on a bill.

What do you call an American drawing?

A Yankee doodle.

What did one flag say to the other?

Nothing. It just waved.

Dad: How is your report card, Maria?

Maria: Well, Dad, I did the same thing as George Washington.

Dad: And what is that?

Maria: I went down in history.

What kind of tea did the American colonists like?

Liberty.

What do presidents eat to freshen their breath?

Govern-mints.

Sara: Did you hear the joke about the Liberty Bell?

Clara: Yeah, it cracked me up!

Knock, knock.

Who's there?

Llama.

Llama who?

"Llama Yankee Doodle Dandy."

Where was the Declaration of Independence signed?

At the bottom.

Why does the Statue of Liberty stand in New York Harbor?

Because she can't sit down.

What was the most popular dance in 1776?

Indepen-dance.

Dezi: If Mrs. Green lives in a green house, Ms. Blue lives in a blue house, and Mr. Red lives in a red house, who lives in the White House?

Kyle: Mr. White?

Dezi: No, the president of the United States!

Halloween

How do you make a witch itch?

Take away the W.

What is a vampire's favorite holiday?

Fangsgiving.

What do monsters put on before they go in the pool?

Sunscream.

Who is the smartest monster?

Frank Einstein.

Knock, knock.

Who's there?

Ghost.

Ghost who?

Ghost to show you don't remember my name!

What kind of dog is like a vampire?

A bloodhound.

What is a spider's favorite picnic food?

Corn on the cobweb.

What did one zombie say to the other?

"Get a life."

What sound does a witch's ceral make?

Snap, cackle, and pop.

Who won the monster beauty contest?

Nobody.

What does a ghost put on its bagel?

Scream cheese.

Knock, knock.

Who's there?

Eerie.

Eerie who?

Eerie is! Come on in.

What's the best way to talk to a monster?

Long distance.

What do you call a skeleton snake?

A rattler.

What do you do with a green monster?

Wait until it repens.

Who is the best dancer at a Halloween party?

The boogieman.

What do you call a lost wolf?

A where-wolf.

Thanksgiving

What's the difference between Thanksgiving and Halloween?

One has gobblers, and the other has goblins.

What smells the best at Thanksgiving dinner?

Your nose.

If April showers bring May flowers, what do May flowers bring?

Pilgrims.

Why do turkeys gobble?

They never learned table manners.

What do you get when you cross a potato with an elephant?

Mashed potatoes.

Tallulah: Turkey, what are you thankful for?

Turkey: Tofu!

In which month did the Puritans come to America?

April. April showers bring Mayflowers.

How is a penny like a turkey sitting on a fence?

Head's on one side, tail's on the other.

What is a math teacher's favorite Thanksgiving dessert?

Pumpkin pi.

What do vampires put on their holiday turkey?

Grave-y.

What is a turkey's favorite dessert?

Cherry gobbler.

How do you make a turkey float?

With two scoops of ice cream, a bottle of root beer, and a turkey.

What kind of music did the Pilgrims like?

Plymouth Rock.

Why did the potato cross the road?

He saw a fork up ahead.

Maura: Would you like some more green beans?

Teddy Bear: No thanks, I'm stuffed.

Decem-*brr* Holidays

Knock, knock.

Who's there?

Delight.

Delight who?

Delight coming from de menorah is beautiful.

What did the mom say to her children on Hanukkah?

"I love you a latke."

Knock, knock.

Who's there?

Oil.

Oil who?

Oil be right back.

What is a bee's favorite holiday?

Honey-kah.

What did one dreidel say to the other dreidel?

"Spin too long since we saw each other."

Knock, knock.

Who's there?

Mayor.

Mayor who?

Mayor Kwanzaa be filled with peace and unity!

What do you call a cat that goes to the beach on Christmas?

Sandy Claws.

What do elves learn in school?

The elf-abet.

What does a fish hang on its door at Christmas?

A coral wreath.

Why was the elf crying?

He stubbed his mistle-toe.

Knock, knock.

Who's there?

Avery.

Avery who?

Avery Merry Christmas to you!

What's the difference between Santa Claus and a dog?

Santa Claus wears a suit and the dog just pants.

What is a tiger's favorite Christmas carol?

"Jungle bells."

Why did the Christmas tree go to the barber?

It needed to be trimmed.

What is an elf's favorite music?

Gift rap.

LAUGH LESSONS

How do bees get to school?

They take the school buzz.

Why did the teacher wear sunglasses in school?

Because his class was so bright.

Will: Would you be mad at me for something I didn't do?

Teacher: Of course not.

Will: That's good, because I forgot to do my homework!

What kind of candy is always tardy for school?

Choco-late.

Why didn't the zombie go to school?

He felt rotten.

What letter of the alphabet has lots of water?

The C.

Knock, knock.

Who's there?

Razor.

Razor who?

Razor hand if you know the answer.

What did the teacher do with the cheese's homework?

He grated it.

Where do astronauts go to study?

The moon-iversity.

Why did the boy eat his homework?

Because the teacher said it was a piece of cake.

Why was the broom late for school?

It over-swept.

How does a karate teacher greet his students?

"Hi-yah!"

Teacher: Where's your homework, Zach?

Zach: I don't have it. My dog ate it.

Teacher: How could your dog eat your homework?

Zach: I fed it to him.

What is the first thing a monkey learns in school?

His ape, B, C's.

What do you say when comforting a grammar teacher?

"There, their, they're."

Why shouldn't you write with a broken pencil?

It's pointless.

What do you get when you cross an algebra class with the prom?

The quadratic formal.

Why did the clock go to the principal's office?

For tocking too much.

Chase: Were the test questions hard?

Cherie: The questions were easy. It was the answers that gave me trouble!

In mathematics, what is the law of the doughnut?

Two halves make a hole.

Mark: Do you like homework?

Marietta: I like nothing better.

What is a witch's favorite subject?

Spelling.

What kind of dance do teachers like best?

Atten-dance.

Why do fish know a lot?

They swim in schools.

Cory: Why aren't you doing well in history?

Rory: Because the teacher keeps asking about things that happened before I was born.

Why is spaghetti the smartest food?

It always uses its noodle.

What did one math book say to the other?

"We've got problems."

Teacher: What is the capital of Washington?

Annie: The W.

What's the worst thing that can happen to a geography teacher?

Getting lost.

Why is Alabama the smartest state in the USA?

Because it has four A's and one B.

Megan: What's the matter?

Maddie: Anything that has mass and weight.

What do math teachers do in the lunchroom?

They divide their lunches with one another.

Who succeeded the first president of the United States?

The second one.

What do you do if a teacher rolls her eyes at you?

Pick them up and roll them back to her.

Who invented fractions?

Henry the 1/4th.

Teacher: What did they do at the Boston Tea Party?

Landon: I don't know—I wasn't invited!

Why didn't the skeleton like recess?

He had no body to play with.

How did Christopher Columbus's men sleep on their ships?

With their eyes shut.

Teacher: Leah, you missed school yesterday.

Leah: Well, to tell you the truth, I didn't miss it that much.

Knock, knock.

Who's there?

Wafer.

Wafer who?

Wafer the bus at the corner.

Principal: Jordan, what have you been doing in class lately?

Jordan: Nothing!

Principal: That's exactly what your teacher said.

Who invented algebra?

An X-pert.

What is a teacher's favorite nation?

Explanation.

Why is arithmetic hard work?

You have to carry all those numerals.

Dad: What did you learn in school today?

Dylan: Not enough. I have to go back tomorrow!